CW00486601

TRAVELLING SO

by the same author

poetry
ZOOM!
XANADU
KID
BOOK OF MATCHES
THE DEAD SEA POEMS
MOON COUNTRY (with Glyn Maxwell)
CLOUDCUCKOOLAND
KILLING TIME
SELECTED POEMS
THE UNIVERSAL HOME DOCTOR

drama
MISTER HERACLES (after Euripides)

prose
ALL POINTS NORTH
LITTLE GREEN MAN

Travelling Songs

SIMON ARMITAGE

faber and faber

First published in 2002
by Faber and Faber Limited
3 Queen Square London WC1N 3AU
Published in the United States by Faber and Faber, Inc.,
an affiliate of Farrar, Straus and Giroux LLC, New York

Photoset by Wilmaset Ltd, Wirral
Printed in England

All rights reserved
© Simon Armitage, 2002

The right of Simon Armitage to be identified as author
of this work has been asserted in accordance with
Section 77 of the Copyright, Designs and Patents Act 1988

*This book is sold subject to the condition that it shall not,
by way of trade or otherwise, be lent, resold, hired out or
otherwise circulated without the publisher's prior consent in
any form of binding or cover other than that in which it is
published and without a similar condition including this
condition being imposed on the subsequent purchaser*

A CIP record for this book
is available from the British Library

ISBN 0–571–21536–X

2 4 6 8 10 9 7 5 3 1

Contents

Acknowledgements

A version of 'I've started to think' was commissioned by the Colne Valley Male Voice Choir and set to music by Goff Richards. 'Well I got me a bike' was commissioned by the Post Office. A version of 'Operation Fresh Fruit Salad' first appeared as part of the Soundings project. 'The Convergence of the Twain' was first read on BBC Radio 4's *Today* programme. 'Leaves on the Line' was commissioned for the Oriana project and set to music by Dominic Muldowney. Versions of 'Money Spider', 'Adam and Eve' and 'Going Up' were first performed in Goldthorpe's Yard as part of Wilson and Wilson's production of *House*.

TRAVELLING SONGS

★

The army drives with its headlights on,
a cop car yodels its siren song,
I'm struck by a field of rape-seed-oil
or oil-seed-rape or whatever it's called

and it's one for the sake of a left-hand driver,
two for a soft-top Alfa Spider,
three for the dream of a bareback rider,
and I'm right behind her.

I'm thinking of Pluto's eccentric orbit,
the forked tail-end of this year's comet.
The critics go mental for Bacon and Freud.
It's healthier grilled but it's tastier fried

and it's one for the sake of a left-hand driver,
two for a soft-top Alfa Spider,
three for the dream of a bareback rider,
and I'm right behind her.

Smoking blow on the open road
with a roach torn out of the Highway Code.
The moon in its heaven, heaving, mooning.
The last wolf in England was killed for its meaning:

one for the sake of a left-hand driver,
two for a soft-top Alfa Spider,
three for the dream of a bareback rider,
and I'm right behind her.

The Following Directions

In the country, the county, the parish, the place,
this is the bay and the beach funnelled into the lane,
this is the kirk-field growing a season of stones,
this is the grit-box for salting the road.

This is the Gulf Stream, this is the weather,
this is the bull with its nose in a ring-pull,
this is the flag and the flagpole over the lintel,
this is the five-bar gate, the dog with the teeth

at the end of its tether. This is the Mace,
this is the price of milk and yesterday's paper,
this is the Lodge and the school and the next farm,
this is the view, looking east, from the top of the hill.

That's the sea-cat, pressing a seam in the waves from port
to port, that there's Scotland on the other shore.
This is the satellite dish on the back wall,
this is the basketball-hoop over the back door.

This is the third left, this is the same car going past
for the third time, this is the sign to the path
that slows to a dead-end after an acre of cows.
This is as much as you know, as far as it goes.

Little No Thing

We had a thing
      we called a name,

that went and came
      before its time,

whose simple pulse
      they couldn't find,

who had no mind
      to think ahead,

whose heart they said
      was left for dead,

whose will to live
      was weeks behind,

who thoughtlessly
      had gone and died.

Now we have no thing
      in our life.

Killing Time #2

Time in the brain cells sweating like a nail bomb,
trouble with the heartbeat spitting like a Sten gun,
  cut to the chase,
  pick up the pace;
no such thing as a walkabout fun-run,
  shoot yourself a glance in the chrome in the day-room,
don't hang about, your running out of space, son.

Red light, stop sign, belly full of road rage,
ticket from the fuzz if you dawdle in the slow lane,
  pull up your socks,
  get out of the blocks;
twelve-hour day-shift grafting at the coal face,
  turning up the gas brings blood to the boat race,
strike with the iron or you're sleeping in the stone age.

Don't dilly dally or the trail goes cold, sir,
don't hold back till you're mouldy old dough, sir,
  sprint for the line,
  turn on a dime;
sit tight, hang fire, I'm putting you on hold, sir,
  too late, snail pace, already sold, sir,
blame it on the kids but it's you getting old, sir.

Short cut, fast track, trolley dash at Quick Save,
four minute warning, boil yourself an egg, babe,
  crack the whip,
  shoot from the hip;
close shave, tear arse, riding on a knife blade,
  twenny-four-seven in the brain-drain rat race,
finger on the pulse but you'd better watch your heart rate.

Cheap thrills, speed kills, pop yourself a pill, mate,
thumb a free ride on amphetamine sulphate,
>run with the pack,
>don't look back;
pedal to the floor when you're burning up the home straight,
>her indoors doesn't want you getting home late,
love's in the freezer and your dinner's in the dog-grate.

Ten to the dozen to the grave from the carry-cot,
bolt like a thoroughbred, talk like a chatterbox,
>oil the wheels,
>pick up your heels;
ginseng tea turns out to be tommyrot,
>reach for the future with a hand full of liver-spots,
fuse-wire burns in the barrel of a body-clock.

Cut yourself in half doing life at the sharp end,
meet your own self coming back around the U-bend,
>get with the beat,
>turn up the heat;
sink like a stone by going off the deep end,
>fifty quid an hour for a top-flight shrink, said
start killing time, it's later than you think, friend.

★

I've started to think
about life on the drink
and I'm sailing out into the blue.
And there's room in the cabin for two.
So float like a cork and then put into port for me,
crew for me, stew for me, boil up a brew for me,
all the way over the sea.

I'm right on the brink
of life on the drink
and I'm sailing out into the blue.
And there's room in the cabin for two.
So stay for me, pray for me, cough up and pay for me,
sob for me, slob for me, break out the grog for me,
jibe for me, tack for me, take up the slack for me,
slurp for me, burp for me, load up a crate for me,
turpentine's great for me,
work up a thirst for me,
put yourself first for me,
bob for me, toss for me, climb on your cross for me,
all the way over the sea.

I've started to sink
into life on the drink
and I'm sailing out into the blue.
And there's room in the cabin for two.
So duck for me, dive for me, bum me a five for me,
dress for me, stress for me, wipe up the mess for me,
pass up the rest for me,
stick out your chest for me,
boke for me, choke for me, crack me a joke for me,
light up a smoke for me,
get out and graft for me,

[8]

rig up a raft for me,
nip for me, tuck for me, ride out your luck for me,
vouch for me, crouch for me, open your pouch for me,
lather me, razor me, Mother Theresa me,
don't ask me why for me,
live me a lie for me,
bleed yourself dry and then sod off and die for me,
all the way over the sea.

The National Trust Range of Paints Colour Card

String and Pigeon and Sugar-Bag Light,
Lichen and Powder Blue.
> *I can sing a rainbow, sing a rainbow,*
> *sing a rainbow too.*

Hay and Biscuit and Hardwick White,
Buff and Berrington Blue.
> *Poverty's a shame though, is a shame though,*
> *is a shame it's true.*

Drab and Olive, Dead Salmon and Bone,
Down Pipe and Ballroom Blue.
> *Nobody's to blame though, is to blame though,*
> *is to blame but you.*

Eating-Room Red and London Stone,
Fowler Pink, Cane and Hague Blue.
> *I can see the grain grow, see the grain grow,*
> *see the grain grow through.*

★

Oh motorway, motorway,
where have you bin,
oh motorway where are you stopping?
I've been down to London
to pick up the King,
to take him up north to go shopping.

Oh bring him to us
for a Pontefract cake
and we'll light up the sky with a rocket.
No I'm taking him home
with the killings he made
with some fluff that he found in his pocket.

★

Well I got me a bike, boy did I get me a bike.
The kind of contraption a bike-o-phobic type person
would not like, with its twenty-five-speed
drop-handlebar-dynamo-quick-release-click-shift-gears
and alloy wheels fore and aft,
and a bell and a pump. Know what?
I was going away like a dream
when somebody shouted *Get off and milk it you great oaf,*
then I woke up, jumped out of bed, and fell off.

So I got me a 'plane, boy did I get me a 'plane.
Wingspan wider than heaven's gate,
body so long it was a bus ride nose to tail;
this mother-of-all-flights was east and west at the same time,
everyone's air-space rolled into one
with water-bed seats and leg-room for people on stilts
and giveaway cocktails twenty-foot long. I should have known:
when the string broke, the kite came down
like a lead balloon, and I had to walk home.

So I got me a train, boy did I get me a train.
Talk about iron horses, this was a whole team
with pistons for legs and a head of steam.
Felt like Pegasus flying the big bridges
over the valleys and gorges. Making up time, I was,
but at twenty past nine I had to pack up,
put the carriages back in their boxes, break up the line,
hang up the hat of the engine driver,
unplug the transformer.

So I got me a boat, oh boy did I get me a boat.
There's only one way to get there and that's to float.
I was only a nautical mile from port

after single-handedly sailing a lap of the world
but had to get out of the tub when the soap disappeared
and the water went cold.

I'm going to post me a note to the gods of the country lane
and the iron road and the clear blue sky
and the open sea. OK, from out there it might look
like going nowhere fast, not going anywhere,

but believe me, I'm getting there.

Operation Fresh Fruit Salad

They probed your eyes with the beam of a torch
but your eyes were unmoved. They stroked them shut.
Your lips were set, mouthing a bubble of spit
like blown glass, blown with a last breath.
    8 oz seedless black grapes blown with a last breath.

Skin would not be provoked, muscle wouldn't flinch.
Your nerves were out cold, wouldn't jerk
to the beat of a hammer, tapped on the rim of the knee.
Your funny bone was dead wood, baffled with flesh.
    The pips of one pomegranate baffled with flesh.

Your nose couldn't rouse the genie of crystallised salt
from its bottled sleep. Jump-starting your heart
didn't work; in shirt-sleeves, they pumped and plunged
with bare hands, but the deadness stayed put.
    2 Cox's apples but the deadness stayed put.

So the cavers went in through the ear, got so far,
called into the space beyond. In front were other worlds:
viaducts of bone, sea-gardens of coral in full bloom,
lunar canals, the juice of a lemon, spiralling

into the core. They could only turn back, or wait.
Then a voice from under the rubble of thought,
buried alive in a pocket of air in the brain
came answering back, crying your own name.
    One small pineapple of air in the brain.
    Tangerine segments crying your own name.

Money Spider

Money-spinner, little dot,
she comes here out of the light,
out from under the feet
down steps that were cut from the rocks of the moon,
likely as not, into this room of stone.
Said to be short of sight,
telling not much more than day from night,
yet look at this fine work:
tapestry, lace and needlepoint,
and nine times out of a dozen she's here,
weaving cloth from snippets of hair,
spinning out thread, darning socks,
tying a blanket of knots,
stringing a harp with dental floss,
lining the sleeves and the pockets of suits
with the ears of pigs and parachute silk.
Said to bring good luck
wherever she sets foot,
she keeps herself to herself, except
on the second Tuesday of every month
when she packs it all up
in a carpet bag, except
the christening shawl and the little blue vest,
and the hand-blown egg
in its cotton wool nest,
and fingers her way
to market day in the market square
and peddles the lot
for chickenfeed, peanuts, pin-money, slack.
Money-spinner, little mite,
the money she makes she cleans and hides
in a hollowed-out book.
And a storm-cloud anchors over the house

when she pulls up a chair and takes from the shelf
that miracle-cure of personal wealth and possible truth
the glory of worth,
and she tries each coin on the tip of her tongue
and it tastes like metal, and blood, and life, and more to come.

★

Adam and Eve, Adam and Eve,
the life we've lived you wouldn't believe.
Accident and emergency,
the agony and the ecstasy.
The road is long and slow and hard
from Paradise to Goldthorpe's Yard.
It breaks the heart
with all the things we've heard and seen
to stay so adamant and evergreen.

Adam and Eve, Adam and Eve,
the life we've lived you wouldn't believe.
Accident and emergency,
the agony and the ecstasy.
(I don't blame her for where we are –
she's Adam's little evening star,
she's Adam's rib for evermore.)
The road is long and slow and hard
from Paradise to Goldthorpe's Yard.
(He's blamed me from the very start –
he stands there in his snakeskin belt,
he sits there eating apple tart.)
It breaks the heart
with all the things we've heard and seen
to stay so adamant and evergreen.

Adam and Eve, Adam and Eve,
the life we've lived you wouldn't believe.
Accident and emergency,
the agony and the ecstasy.
The road is long and slow and hard
from Paradise to Goldthorpe's Yard.
It breaks the heart
with all the things we've heard and seen
to stay so adamant and evergreen.

Going Up

Lived in a boot.
Hand-made calf-skin, fitted dead snug.
Rolled down tongue so it was open-top.
Jehovah's Witnesses didn't know where to knock.
Not 100% waterproof but good enough.
Drank beer over garden wall of ankle cuff.
Lived in a boot.

Lived in a boot.
Peered through eyelets
like a sailor coming into port.
Picnicked outside on toe-end like it was Castle Hill.
Salt mark – like tide mark around bath – wouldn't come off.
No fucker visited, but so what?
Lived in a boot.

Lived in a boot.
Pulled laces tight on nights with no moon.
Kept loaded twelve-bore in hollowed-out heel.
More and more neighbours in slip-ons and brogues.
Less and less walks, stayed home to keep guard.
Lived in a boot.

Lived in a boot.
Wore down on one side – started to rock.
Scuff marks and cracks, polish and dubbin – couldn't be faffed.
Toxocariasis from shit from dogs – owners should be shot.
Leather went saggy like an old face, nails came through.
Stitching rotted around welt, insoles went manky,
smelt.

Didn't do any more, didn't suit.
Moved out. Moved to a hat.

★

I took a train to Oxford, and walked in to a den
of disappointing poets, and disappointed men.
My father was a stone, I said,
my mother was a hen,
there's who knows what inside my head
but I write like a dream my friends, my friends,
I write like a dream, I said.

I took a train to Cambridge, and walked into the lives
of disappointing teachers and their disappointed wives.
My sister was a bone, I said,
my brother was a gem,
my best day's work was done in bed
but I write like a dream my friends, my friends,
I write like a dream, I said.

I took a plane to Harvard, I took a plane to Yale,
and every student handed in a sorry little tale.
My maker was a star, I said,
my teacher was a mole,
one of these days I'll wake up dead
but I write like a dream my friends, my friends,
I write like a dream, I said.

The Convergence of the Twain

I

Here is an architecture of air.
Where dust has cleared,
nothing stands but free sky, unlimited and sheer.

II

Smoke's dark bruise
has paled, soothed
by wind, dabbed at and eased by rain, exposing the wound.

III

Over the spoil of junk,
rescuers prod and pick,
shout into tangled holes. What answers back is aftershock.

IV

All land lines are down.
Reports of mobile phones
are false. One half-excoriated Apple Mac still quotes the Dow Jones.

V

Shop windows are papered
with faces of the disappeared.
As if they might walk from the ruins – chosen, spared.

VI

With hindsight now we track
the vapour-trail of each flight-path
arcing through blue morning, like a curved thought.

VII

And in retrospect plot
the weird prospect
of a passenger plane beading an office-block.

VIII

But long before dawn,
with those towers drawing
in worth and name to their full height, an opposite was forming,

IX

a force
still years and miles off,
yet moving headlong forwards, locked on a collision course.

X

Then time and space
contracted, so whatever distance
held those worlds apart thinned to an instant.

XI

During which, cameras framed
moments of grace
before the furious contact wherein earth and heaven fused.

Leaves on the Line

In the past he was coming by steam and coal,
by breath of water, flame of stone;
we waited for hours then buggered off home.

    Till Leaf Man come
    how long, how long?

At present he comes by diesel or spark;
with an ear to the rail we can hear him talk.
We wait all day then die in the dark.

    How sung, how sung
    the Leaf Man song?

Tomorrow he'll come on a beam of light,
rise like morning, end this wait,
but the rooster croaked and he's already late.

    Till Leaf Man come, how long, how long,
    how sung, how sung the Leaf Man song?

The Way

It's a short walk from the house of a friend,
the Way, and leads only from here to there,
from its starting point to its very end.

It forms a switchback two spans wide at most.
Its length is possibly measured in strides,
though far too long to bother to keep count –

    all the way in,
    all the way out –

or measured in minutes – the time it takes
to travel the Way at an even pace.
It begins as a stile, ends as a gate.

Going out, to the right side of the Way
is a fence overcome by undergrowth,
and below the banking a railway line,

and freight trains have been known to shuttle through
causing animal life to freeze or move,
plant life to juggle or cling to its fruit –

    all the way down,
    all the way up.

Overdue blackberries, heavy with blood.
Some bird under cover of grass, half choked,
coughs up the sound of the frog in its throat –

    the way down,
    the way up.

To the left side of the Way, going out,
is a field of barley, standing its ground.
So on the home leg, these things turn around.

What grand garden the Way would be, green lane
rolled out from a doorstep in a straight line.
What great lawn, and a long-by-narrow job –

      day long,
      all the day long –

with a motorised blade to keep it so cropped
and shorn. A tractor, dragging a cutter,
would see to the work in a single pass,

but there are no tracks. No footprints either,
as if each step took back the mark it made.
We are all as different as we are the same.

The Way at first light or just before dusk,
deserted of course, except for yourself
of course, and a black dog ranging forward

      and back,
      all the way forward

and back, bringing sticks and stones in its mouth
like memories of the future, premonitions
of the past. De-cap this morning's mushroom

with a toe-poke of the boot, or don't;
tonight, take home a token of the place –
pick out a plant that answers to its name.

      Away home.
      All the way home.

Or the Way, just so, whose opposite form
is a cluster of trees, willows perhaps,
or a field in fallow, going to grass.

It is this state of in-between that counts.
So to claim that the Way is something more
than its parts is a full twist of the facts –

    all the way there,
    the way back –

but to spend time on its strip, come about
on its stretch – that's the stuff – and a good case
could be made for saying at least as much.